TRADITIONAL FOLKSONGS & BALLADS OF
SCOTLAND

40 COMPLETE SONGS, COLLECTED, ARRANGED AND EDITED BY
John Loesberg

Volume Three

Ossian
Cork
Glasgow
Loughborough
New Hampshire

D0274125

OSSIAN PUBLICATIONS LTD. IRELAND
(Publishing Dept.)
P.O. Box 84, Cork

OSSIAN PUBLICATIONS SCOTLAND
9 Rosebery Crescent
Edinburgh EH12 5JP

OSSIAN PUBLICATIONS U.K
Unit 3, Prince William Rd.
Loughborough

OSSIAN PUBLICATIONS USA
RR8 Box 374
Loudon, New Hampshire
03301

OMB 95
ISBN 0 946005 80 X

There was a sang
That aye I wad be singin'
There was a star
An' clear it used tae shine;
An' liltin' in the starlicht
Thro' the shadows
I gaed lang syne.

from 'There was a sang'
Helen B. Cruickshank

The Four Maries

♩. = 58

Yes - treen the Queen had four Ma - ries, The night she'll hae but three; There's Ma - ry Sea - ton an' Ma - ry Bea - ton, An' Ma - ry Car - mich- ael an' me.

Oh, often hae I dress'd my Queen,
An' put gowd in her hair,
But noo I've gotten for my reward
The gallows to be my share

Oh, little did my mither ken,
The day she cradled me,
The land I was to travel in,
The death I was to dee.

Oh, happy, happy is the maid
That's born o' beauty free:
It was my dimplin rosy cheeks
That's been the dule o' me.

OMB 95

Drumdelgie

♩. = 76

There's a fairm - er up in Cairn - ie; Wha's kent baith faur an'
wide, Tae be the great Drum - del - gie Up-
on sweet De - ve - ron side. The fair - mer o' yon
muck - le toon, He is baith hard an' sair, And the
caul - dest day that ev - er blaws, His ser - vants get their
share. Sae fare ye weel Drum - del - gie for
Chorus: Sae fare ye weel Drum - del - gie I
I maun gang a - wa' Sae fare ye weel Drum-
bid you all a - dieu, I leave you as I

del - gie, Your wee - ty wea - ther an' a'.
got you, A maist un - ci - vil crew!

At five o' clock we quickly rise, and hurry doon the stair;
It's there to corn our horses, likewise to straik their hair.
Syne after working half an hour, each to the kitchen goes,
It's there to get our breakfast, which generally is brose.

We've scarcely got our brose weel supt, and gie'en oor pints a tie,
When the foreman cries: 'Hallo my lads, the hour is drawing nigh'.
At sax o'clock the mull's put on, to gie us a strait wark;
It tak's four o' us to mak' for her, till ye could wring our sark.

And when the water is put aff, we hurry doon the stair
To get some quarters through the fan, till daylight does appear.
When daylight does begin to peep, and the sky begins to clear,
The foreman he cries out: 'My lads, Ye'll stay nae langer here !'

'There's sax o' you'll gae to the ploo, and twa will drive the neeps,
And the owsen they'll be after you, wi' strae raips roun' their queets.'
But when that we were gyaun furth, and turnin' out to yoke,
The snaw dank on sae thick and fast, that we were like to choke.

The frost had been sae very hard, the ploo she wadna go;
And sae our cairting days commenced, amang the frost and snow.
Our horses being but young and sma', the shafts they didna fill,
And they aft required the saiddler, to pull them up the hill.

But we will sing our horses' praise, though they be young and sma',
They far outshine the Broadland's anes, that gang sae full and braw.
Sae fare ye weel Drumdelgie, for I maun gang awa;
Sae fare ye weel Drumdelgie, your weety weather and a'.

OMB 95

Ye Banks and Braes

Ye banks and braes o' bon-nie Doon, How can ye bloom sae fresh and fair? How can ye chant, ye lit-tle birds And I sae wea-ry, fu' o' care. Thou'll break my heart, thou warb-ling birds, That wan-tons through the flow'-ring thorn; Thou minds me o' de-part-ed joys, De-part-ed ne-ver to re-turn.

Aft hae I rov'd by Bonnie Doon,
To see the rose and woodbine twine:
And ilka bird sang o' its luve,
And fondly sae did I o' mine.
Wi' lightsome heart I pu'd a rose,
Fu' sweet upon its thorny tree !
And my fause luver staw my rose,
But ah ! he left the thorn wi' me.

Loch Lomond

We'll meet where we parted in yon shady glen,
On the steep, steep side o' Ben Lomond,
Where in purple hue the Hieland hills we view,
And the moon looks out frae the gloamin.

Chorus

O brave Charlie Stuart ! dear true the true heart,
Wha could refuse thee protection
Like the weeping birch on the wild hillside,
How graceful he looked in dejection !

Chorus

The wild birdies sing and the wild flowers spring,
An' in sunshine the waters are sleepin;'
But the broken heart it kens, nae second spring,
Tho' the waefu' may cease frae their greetin' !

Chorus

OMB 95

The Bonnie Hoose o' Airlie

♩ = 84

1. It fell on a day, a bon-nie sim-mer day, When the
4. corn grew green and yel - low, That there fell out a
7. great dis-pute Be-tween Ar-gyle and Air - lie. The
10. Duke o' Mont - rose has writ-ten to Ar-gyle, To
12. come in the morn - in' ear - ly, An'
14. lead on his men by the back o' Dun-keld, To
16. plun-der the bon - nie hoose o' Air - lie.

The lady look'd o'er her window sae hie, —
And, oh ! but she look'd weary, —
And there she espied the great Argyle
Come to plunder the bonnie hoose o' Airlie.
'Come doun, come doun, Lady Margaret,' he says,
Come doun and kiss me fairly,
Or before the mornin' clear daylight,
I'll no leave a standin' stane in Airlie.'

'I wadna kiss thee, great Argyle,
I wadna kiss thee fairly;
I wadna kiss thee, great Argyle,
Gin ye shoulna leave a standin' stane in Airlie.'
He has ta'en her by the middle sae sma',
Says: 'Lady, where is your drury ?'
'It's up and doun the bonnie burn side,
Amang the plantin' o' Airlie.'

They sought it up, and they sought it down,
They sought it late and early,
And found it in the bonnie balm-tree,
That shines in the bowlin' green o' Airlie.
He has ta'en her by the left shoulder, —
And oh ! but she grat sairly, —
And led her down to yon green bank,
Till he plundered the bonnie hoose o' Airlie.

'Oh ! it's I ha'e seven braw sons,' she says,
And the youngest ne'er saw his daddie,
And although I had as mony mae,
I wad gie them a' to Charlie.
But gin my good lord had been at hame,
As this night he is wi' Charlie,
There durst na a Campbell in a' the west
Ha'e plundered the bonnie hoose o' Airlie.'

O My Love is like a Red, Red Rose

Till a' the seas gang dry, my dear,
And the rocks melt wi' the sun;
And I will luve thee still, my dear,
While the sands o' life shall run.

And fare-thee-weel, my only luve !
And fare-thee-weel a while !
And I will come again, my luve,
Tho' it were ten thousand mile.

Mingulay Boat Song

♩ = 63

F
Hill you ho, boys, Let her go boys; Bring her

C   3   Bb
head round, now all to-ge - ther. Hill you

F
ho, boys; Let her go, boys; Sail - ing

C   3   F
home, home to Ming - u - lay.

What care we though white the Minch is ?
What care we for wind or weather ?
Let her go boys ! ev'ry inch is
Wearing home, home to Mingulay.

Chorus

Wives are waiting on the bank,or
Looking seaward from the heather;
Pull her round boys ! and we'll anchor,
Ere the sun sets at Mingulay.

Chorus

13

OMB 95

The Dowie Dens o' Yarrow

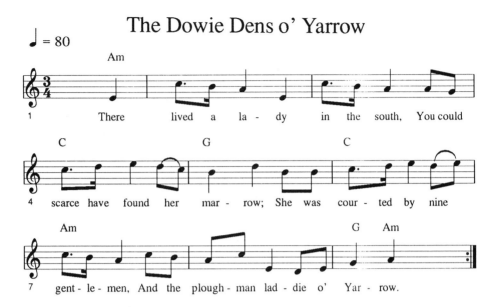

There lived a lady in the south, You could
scarce have found her mar - row; She was cour - ted by nine
gent - le - men, And the plough - man lad - die o' Yar - row.

As he came ower yon high, high hill,
And down yon glen so narrow,
There he spied nine gentlemen
Come to fight with him on Yarrow.

If I see all, there's nine to ane,
And that's an unequal marrow;
But I will take you three by three,
And I'll slay you all on Yarrow.

Then three he slew, and three withdrew,
And three lay deadly wounded,
Till her brother John stepped in behind
And pierced his body through.

Go home, go home, ye false young man,
And tell your sister sorrow,
That her true love John lies dead and gone
In the dowie dens o' Yarrow.

As she came ower yon high, high hill,
And down yon glen so narrow,
It's there she spied her brother John
Returning home from Yarrow.

O brother dear, I've dreamt a dream,
And I fear it will prove sorrow,
For I dreamt that you were spilling blood
In the dowie dens o' Yarrow.

O sister dear, I'll read your dream,
And I'm sure it will prove sorrow,
Your true love John lies dead and gone,
A bloody corpse in Yarrow.

She wrung her hands and tore her hair,
Wi' muckle grief and sorrow,
For she dearly loved her true love John,
The ploughman laddie o' Yarrow.

This lady's hair being three-quarters long,
And the colour of it was yellow,
She's tied it round her middle jimp,
And she carried him home from Yarrow.

O daughter, dear, dry up your tears,
And dwell no more in sorrow,
And I'll wed you to one of a higher degree
Than the ploughman laddie o' Yarrow.

O father, ye hae seven sons,
Ye can wed them a' tomorrow,
But a fairer flower than my true love John
There never bloomed in Yarrow.

Now this lady, she being in distress,
For her love who died on Yarrow,
She flung herself in her father's arms,
And died through grief and sorrow.

OMB 95

Henry Martin

The lot it fell upon Henry Martin,
The youngest of all the three,
That he should turn robber all on the salt sea,
    salt sea, salt sea,
For to maintain his two brothers and he.

He had not been sailing but a long winter's night,
And part of a short winter's day,
When he espied a lofty stout ship,
    stout ship, stout ship,
Come a-bibing down on him straightway.

'Hello, hello', cried Henry martin,
'What makes you sail so high?''
'I'm a rich merchant ship bound for fair London Town,
    London Town, London Town,
Will you please for to let me pass by?'

'O no, O no', cried Henry Martin,
'That thing it never can be,
For I have turned robber all on the salt sea,
    salt sea, salt sea,
For to maintain my two brothers and me'.

So lower your topsail and brail up your mizzen,
Bow yourselves under my lee,
Or I shall give you a fast flowing ball,
    flowing ball, flowing ball,
And your dear bodies drown in the salt sea'.

With broadside and broadside and at it they went
For fully two hours or three,
Till Henry Martin gave to her the death shot,
    the death shot, the death shot.
Heavily listing to starboard went she.

The rich merchant vessel was wounded full sore,
Straight to the bottom went she,
And Henry Martin sailed away on the sea,
    salt sea, salt sea,
For to maintain his two brothers and he.

Bad new, bad news, to old England came
Bad news to fair London Town,
There was a rich vessel and she's cast away,
    Cast away, cast away,
And all of her merry men drowned.

OMB 95

The Deil's Awa' wi' th'Exciseman

We'll mak our maut, and we'll brew our drink,
We'll laugh, sing, and rejoice, man,
And mony braw thanks to the meikle black deil,
That danc'd awa wi' th' Exciseman.

Chorus

There's threesome reels, there's foursome reels,
There's hornpipes and strathspeys, man,
But the ae best dance ere came to the land
Was 'The deil's awa wi' the' Exciseman.'

Chorus

My Donald

♩ = 100

My Do- nald he works on the sea, Wi' the
wind blow -in' wild an' free He
spli- ces the ropes and he sets the sails Then
he's a- wa' to the hame o' the whale

He ne'er thinks o' me far behind
Or the torments that rage in my mind.
He's mine for only half part o' the year,
Then I'm left alane wi' nocht but a tear.

Ye ladies wha smell o' wild rose
Think ye for your perfume to whaur a man goes.
Think ye o' the wives an' the bairnies wha yearn
For a man ne'er returned frae huntin' the sperm.

Repeat first verse

OMB 95

A Pair o' Nicky Tams

♩. = 88

Fan I was bare-ly ten years auld, I left the pa-rish schweel. My fai-ther fee'd me tae The Mains tae chaw his milk and meal. First I pit on my nar-row breeks tae hap my spin-nel trams. Syne buck-led 'roon my knap-pin knees a pair o' nic-ky tams

First I gaed on for Baillie loon and syne gaed on for third
And syne of course I had tae get the horseman's grip an' word,
A loaf o' breid tae be my piece an' a bottle for drinkin' drams,
Ye could nae gang through the calf house door without your nicky tams.

The fairmer I am wi' eynoo he's wealthy but he's mean.
Though corn is cheap his horse is poor, his harness fairly deen.
He gars us load our carts ower fou, his conscience has nae qualms,
Fan breist straps break there's naethin' like a pair of' nicky tams.

I'm courtin' bonnie Annie noo, Rob Tamson's kitchie deem,
She is five and forty and I am seventeen.
She clorts a muckle piece tae me wi' different kinds o' jams,
And tells me ilka nicht how she admires my nicky tams.

I startit oot ae Sunday morn the kirkie for tae gang
My collar it was unco tight, my breeks were nane ower lang,
I had my Bible in my pooch, likewise my book o' Psalms,
When Annie roared :'Ye muckle gowk! tak off your nicky tams!'

Though unco sweer, I took them off, the lassie for tae please
And syne of course, my breeks they lirkit up aroon' my knees,
A wasp gaed crawlin' up my leg in the middle o' the psalms
Oh never again will I ride the kirk wi' oot my nicky tams!

OMB 95

Mairi's Wedding

♩ = 100

G   Em   C   D

1 Step we gai - ly, on we go, heel for heel and toe for toe,

G   Em   C   D

3 Arm in arm and row on row, All for Mai - ri's wed - ding.

G   Em   C   D

5 Ov- er hill ways up and down, Myrt - le green and brack- en brown,

G   Em   C   D

7 Past the shie - lings, thro' the town; All for sake of Mai - ri.

Chorus

Red her cheeks as rowans are,
Bright her eye as any star,
Fairest o' them a' by far
Is our darling Mairi.

Chorus

Plenty herring, plenty meal,
Plenty peat to fill her creel,
Plenty bonny bairns as weel;
That's the toast for Mairi.

Chorus

The Braes o' Killiecrankie

♩ = 72

1 Whaur hae ye been sae braw, lad, Whaur hae ye been sae

5 bran - kie - o? Whaur hae ye been sae braw, lad? Cam'

8 ye by Kil - lie - cran - kie - o. An' ye had been whaur

12 I hae been, Ye wad - na been sae cam - tie - o; An ye had seen what

16 I hae seen i' the braes o' Kil - lie - cran - kie - o.

2 I fought at land, I fought at sea,
At hame I fought my auntie, O;
But I met the devil and Dundee
On the braes o' Killiecrankie, O.

Chorus

3 The bauld Pitcur fell in a furr,
And Clavers gat a clankie, O,
Or I had fed an Athol gled
On the braes o' Killiecrankie, O.

Chorus

4 Oh, fie, Mackay! what gart ye lie
In the bush ayont the brankie, O;
Ye'd better kiss'd King Willie's loof,
Than come to Killiecrankie, O.

Final Chorus:
It's nae shame, it's nae shame,
It's nae shame tae shank ye, O;
There's sour slaes on Athol braes,
And deils at Killiecrankie, O.

OMB 95

The Glencoe Massacre

♩ = 76

O, dark loured the night o'er the wild moun - tain heath, The wild ra- ven's croaked out the bo - dings of death, While Flo - ra, poor Flo - ra, she wan der'd in woe, To seek for Mac Don - ald, the pride of Glen- coe.

While sweet balmy sleep closed each eye in rest
And the chieftain slumbered with peace in his breast,
Ne'er dreading the hour that fate seem'd to show,
That bloody and pale he should lie in Glencoe.

But a flash soon denoted the signal was given,
And the thunders of death wak'd the meteors of Heav'n,
While Flora, poor Flora, she wandered in woe,
To seek for McDonald, the pride of Glencoe.

Oh! sudden a flash on her vision did glare,
While a cannon's loud thunder was pealed through the air,
It wakened ten thousand brave heroes below,
And roared through the caverns of mighty Glencoe.

The smoke then arose from our dear native glen,
With the shrieks of the women and the cries of the men,
Naked mothers were shot with their babes as they ran,
For the English had risen to murder the clan.

Oh, many a warrior that evening was slain,
While the blaze of the village gleam'd far o'er the plain,
Five hundred McDonalds that night were laid low
And their blood stained the heath of their native Glencoe.

© 1994, Ossian Publications Ltd. World Copyright

Then Flora she shriek'd while loose hung her hair,
O, where is my Donald, O tell me, O where;
The tempest's loud torrents o'er the mountains do blow;
And stretch'd cold and bloody he lies in Glencoe.

When a sigh of despair then arose from her breast,
And memory soon told her he slumbered at rest,
He slumbers for ever now free from his woe,
And left his loved Flora, the pride of Glencoe.

Her dark rolling eyes then did kindle like fire,
She fell on his body and then did expire;
No more lovely Flora again feared her woe,
But in death found her Donald, the pride of Glencoe.

Now over their heads the green grass does wave,
And the wild flowers do nod o'er their desolate grave,
And the strangers at the pass shed a tear as they go,
For Flora and Donald, the pride of Glencoe.

OMB 95

Scots Wha Hae

♩ = 84

Scots, wha hae wi' Wal- lace bled, Scots, wham Bruce has af- ten led,

Wel-come to your go- ry bed, Or to vic- to- rie !

Now's the day, and now's the hour; See the front o' bat- tle lour;

See ap-proach proud Ed- ward's pow'r, Chains and sla- ve- rie !

Wha will be a traitor knave ?
Wha can fill a coward's grave ?
Wha sae base as be a slave ?
       Let him turn and flee !
Wha, for Scotland's King and Law,
Freedom's sword will strongly draw,
Freeman stand, or Freeman fa',
       Let him on wi' me !

By Oppression's woes and pains !
By your sons in servile chains !
We will drain our dearest veins,
       But they shall be free !
Lay the proud Usurpers low !
Tyrants fall in every foe !
Liberty's in every blow !__
       Let us do or die !

The Scottish Emigrant's Fareweel

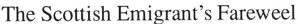

Fare-weel, fare-weel, my na-tive hame, Thy lone-ly glens an' heath-clad moun-tains, Fare-weel, thy fields o' sto-ried fame, Thy leaf-y shaws an' spark-lin' foun-tains. Nae mair I'll climb the Pent-land's steep, Nor wan-der by the Esk's clear ri-ver; I seek a hame far o'er the deep, My na-tive land, fare-weel for e-ver.

Thou land wi' love an' freedom crowned—
In ilk wee cot an' lordly dwellin'
May manly-hearted youths be found,
And maids in ev'ry grace excellin'—
The land where Bruce and Wallace wight
For freedom fought in days o' danger,
Ne'er crouch'd to proud usurpin' might,
But foremost stood, wrong's stern avenger.

Tho' far frae thee, my native shore,
An' toss'd on life's tempestuous ocean;
My heart, aye Scottish to the core,
Shall cling to thee wi' warm devotion.
An' while the wavin' heather grows,
An' onward rows the winding river,
The toast be 'Scotland's broomy knowes,
Her mountains, rocks, an' glens for ever!'

OMB 95

The Gallowa' Hills

For I say 'bonnie lassie it's will ye come wi' me
Tae share your lot in a strange country
For tae share your lot when doon fa's a'
An' I'll gang oot ower the hills tae Gallowa.'

Chorus

For I'll sell my rock, I'll sell my reel,
I'll sell my granny's spinning wheel
I will sell them a' when doon fa's a'
An' I'll gang oot ower the hills tae Gallowa.'

Chorus

OMB 95

Johnny Lad

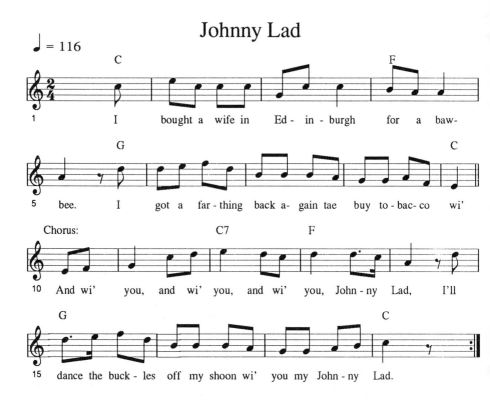

♩ = 116

I bought a wife in Ed-in-burgh for a baw-
bee. I got a far-thing back a-gain tae buy to-bac-co wi'

Chorus:
And wi' you, and wi' you, and wi' you, John-ny Lad, I'll
dance the buck-les off my shoon wi' you my John-ny Lad.

As I was walking early, I chanced to see the Queen,
She was playing at the fitba' wi' the lads in Glasgow Green.

Chorus

The captain of the ither side was scoring wi' great style,
So the Queen she cried a polisman and she clapped him in the jyle.

Chorus

Noo Samson was a michty man, he focht wi' cuddies' jaws,
And he won a score o' battles wearing crimson flannel drawers.

Chorus

There was a man o' Nineveh and he was wondrous wise,
He louped intae a bramble bush and scratched oot baith his eyes.

Chorus

And when he saw his eyes wis oot he wis gey troubled ther.
So he louped intae anither bush and scratched them in again.

Chorus

Noo Johnny is a bonny lad, he is a lad o' mine.
I've never had a better lad and I've had twenty-nine

Chorus

Duncan Gray

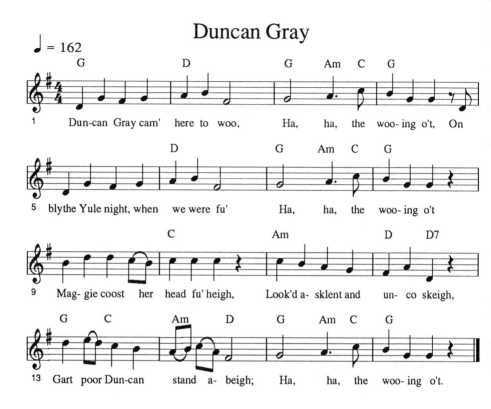

♩ = 162

1 Dun-can Gray cam' here to woo, Ha, ha, the woo- ing o't, On

5 blythe Yule night, when we were fu' Ha, ha, the woo- ing o't

9 Mag- gie coost her head fu' heigh, Look'd a- sklent and un- co skeigh,

13 Gart poor Dun-can stand a- beigh; Ha, ha, the woo- ing o't.

2 Duncan fleech'd and Duncan pray'd;
Ha, ha, the wooing o't,
Meg was deaf as Ailsa craig,
Ha, ha, the wooing o't:
Duncan sigh'd baith out and in,
Grat his een baith blear'd and blin',
Spak o' lowpin o'er a linn;
Ha, ha, the wooing o't.

3 Time and Chance are but a tide,
Ha, ha the wooing o't,
Slighted love is sair to bide,
Ha, ha, the wooing o't:
'Shall I like a fool,' quoth he,
'For a haughty hizzie die ?
She may gae to — France for me !'
Ha, ha, the wooing o't.

4 How it comes let doctors tell,
Ha, ha, the wooing o't;
Meg grew sick, as he grew hale,
Ha, ha, the wooing o't.
Something in her bosom wrings,
For relief a sigh she brings:
And O ! her een they spak sic things !
Ha, ha ,the wooing o't.

5 Duncan was a lad o' grace,
Ha, ha,the wooing o't:
Maggie's was a piteous case,
Ha, ha, the wooing o't:
Duncan could na be her death,
Swelling Pity smoor'd his wrath;
Now they're crouse and canty baith,
Ha, ha, the wooing o't.

The Sun Rises Bright in France

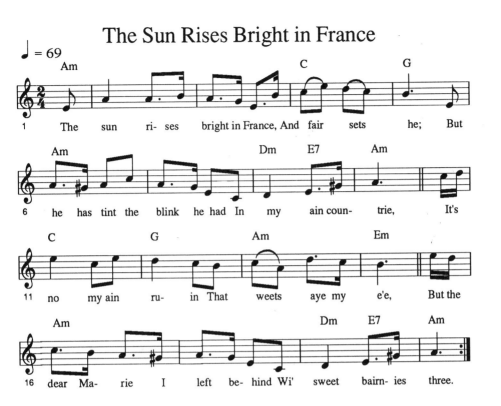

The bud comes back to summer,
And the blossom to the tree,
But I win back—oh, never,
To my ain countrie.
Gladness comes to many,
Sorrow comes to me,
As I look o'er the wide ocean
To my ain countrie.

Fu' bienly low'd my ain hearth.
And smiled my ain Marie:
Oh ! I've left my heart behind
In my ain countrie !
O I'm leal to high heaven,
Which aye was leal to me !
And it's there I'll meet ye a' soon,
Frae my ain countrie.

OMB 95

The Flowers of the Forest

♩ = 76

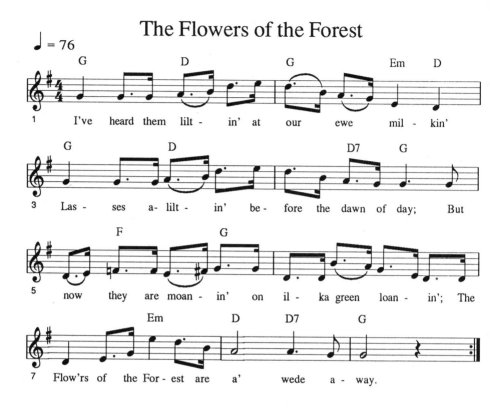

1 I've heard them lilt - in' at our ewe mil - kin'

3 Las - ses a - lilt - in' be - fore the dawn of day; But

5 now they are moan - in' on il - ka green loan - in'; The

7 Flow'rs of the For - est are a' wede a - way.

At buchts in the morning, nae blythe lads are scorning,
The lasses are lonely, and dowie, and wae;
Nae daffin', nae gabbin', but sighing and sabbing,
Ilk ane lifts her leglen and hies away.

In hairst, at the shearing, nae youths now are jeering,
The bandsters are lyart, and runkled and grey;
At fair, or at preaching, nae wooing, nae fleeching—
The Flowers o' the Forest are a' wede away.

At e'en, at the gloaming, nae swankies are roaming,
'Bout stacks wi' the lasses at bogle to play;
But ilk ane sits drearie, lamenting her dearie—
The Flowers o' the Forest are a' wede away.

Dule and wae to the order, sent our lads to the border !
The English, for aince, by guile wan the day;
The Flowers o' the Forest, that foucht aye the foremost,
The pride o' our land, are cauld in the clay.

We hear nae mair lilting at our yowe-milking,
Women and bairns are heartless and wae;
Sighing and moaning on ilka green loaning—
The Flowers o' the Forest are a' wede away.

The Winter it is Past

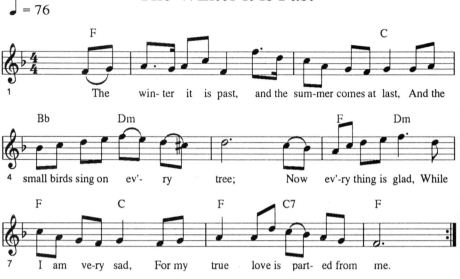

♩ = 76

The winter it is past, and the summer comes at last, And the
small birds sing on ev'- ry tree; Now ev'-ry thing is glad, While
I am ve-ry sad, For my true love is part- ed from me.

The rose upon the brier, by the waters running clear,
May have charms for the linnet or the bee;
Their little loves are blest, and their little hearts at rest,
But my true love is parted from me.

My love is like the sun, that in the sky does run
For ever so constant and true;
But his is like the moon, that wanders up and doun,
And every month it is new.

All you that are in love, and cannot it remove,
I pity the pains you endure;
For experience makes me know that your hearts are full of woe,
A woe that no mortal can cure.

Oh Charlie, Oh Charlie

♩ = 88

Am / **G**

1. Oh Char- lie, Oh Char- lie, come owre frae Pit- gair, And

Am / **Em** / **G Am** / **G**

4. I'll gie ye out all your or- ders, For I maun a- wa to yon

C / **G** / **Am** / **Em** / **G Am**

7. high Hie-lan' hills, For a while to leave the bon-nie Buch-an bor-ders.

Oh Charlie, Oh Charlie, tak' notice what I say,
And put every man to his station,
For I'm gaun awa' to yon high Hielan' hills,
For to view a' the pairts o' the nation.

To the loosin' ye'll put Shaw, ye'll put Sandison to ca',
To the colin ye'll put auld Andrew Kindness,
Ye'll gar auld Colliehill aye feed the thrashin' mill,
An' see that he dee't wi' great fineness.

To the gatherin' o' the hay ye'll put little Isa Grey,
And wi' her ye'll put her cousin Peggy;
And in aneath the bands, it's there ye'll put your hands,
And ye'll see that they dee't richt tidy.

As for you, Willie Burr, ye'll carry on the stir,
And ye'll keep a' the lasses a-hyowin',
And beware o' Shaw and Jeck, or they'll play you a trick,
And set a' your merry maids a-mowin'.

And for you Annie Scott, ye'll put on the muckle pot,
And ye'll mak' milk pottage a-plenty,
For yon hungry brosers that's comin' frae Pitgair,
They're keepit aye sae bare and scanty.

Oh Charlie, Oh Charlie, sae early you'll rise,
And see a' my merry men yokin';
And you, Missy Pope, ye'll sit in the parlour neuk
And keep a' my merry men frae smokin'.

OMB 95

Farewell to Fiunary

A thousand, thousand tender ties—
Accept this day my plaintive sighs;
My heart within me almost dies
At thought of leaving Fiunary.

Chorus

With pensive steps I've often stroll'd
Where Fingal's castle stood of old,
And listen'd while the shepherds told
The legend tales of Fiunary.

Chorus

I've often paused at close of day
Where Ossian sang his martial lay
And viewed the sun's departing ray,
When wandr'ing o'er Fiunary.

Chorus

'Tis not the hills nor wooded vales
Alone my joyless heart bewails,
A mournful group this day remains
Within the manse of Fiunary.

Chorus

O, must I leave these happy scenes ?
See, they spread the flapping sails,
Adieu, adieu ! my native plains;
Farewell to Fiunary !

Chorus

39

Leezie Lindsay

♩ = 108

To gang to the Hielands wi' you, sir,
I dinna ken how that may be,
For I ken na' the land that ye live in,
Nor ken I the lad I'm gaun wi'.

O Leezie, lass, ye maun ken little
If sae be that ye dinna ken me;
My name is Lord Ronald MacDonald,
A chieftain o' high degree.

She has kilted her coats o' green satin,
She has kilted them up to the knee;
And she's aff wi' Lord Ronald MacDonald,
His bride and his darling to be.

Coulter's Candy

♩ = 132

Al- ly, Bal- ly   Al-ly Bal-ly Bee,   Sit- tin' on   yer   mam-my's knee.

Gree- tin' for   a   wee baw- bee,   Tae   buy some Coul-ter's   Can-dy

Puir wee Jeannie she's lookin' affa' thin
A rickle o' banes covered ower wi' skin
Noo she's gettin' a wee double chin
Wi' sookin' Coulter's candy.

Here's auld Coulter comin' roon'
Wi' a basket on his croon
So here's a penny, noo ye rin doon
And buy some Coulter's candy.

Ally, bally, ally, bally bee,
When ye grow up ye'll gang tae sea
Makin' pennies for your daddie and me
Tae buy some Coulter's candy.

OMB 95

Bonnie Strathyre

Then there's mirth in the sheiling and love in my breast,
When the sun is gane doun and the kye are at rest;
For there's mony a prince wad be proud to aspire
To my winsome wee Maggie, the pride o' Strathyre.
Her lips are like rowans in ripe simmer seen,
And mild as the starlight the glint o' her e'en;
Far sweeter her breath than the scent o' the briar,
And her voice is sweet music in bonnie Strathyre.

Set Flora by Colin, and Maggie by me,
And we'll dance to the pipes swellin' loudly and free,
Till the moon in the heavens climbing higher and higher
Bids us sleep on fresh brackens in bonnie Strathyre.
Though some in the touns o' the Lawlands seek fame
And some will gang sodgerin' far from their hame;
Yet I'll aye herd my cattle, and bigg my ain byre,
And love my ain Maggie in bonnie Strathyre.

43

Turn Ye To Me

The waves are dancing merrily, merrily,
Ho ro Mhaire dhu, turn ye to me;
The sea-birds are wailing, wearily, wearily,
Ho ro Mhairi dhu, turn ye to me.
Hushed be thy moaning, lone bird of the sea,
Thy home on the rocks is a shelter to thee,
Thy home is the angry wave,
Mine but the lonely grave,
Ho ro Mhairi dhu, turn ye to me.

45

Ye Canna Shove Yer Granny

♩ = 108

Oh ye can- na shove yer gran- ny aff a bus, Push!

Push! Oh ye can- na shove yer gran- ny aff a bus, Push!

Push! Oh ye can- na shove yer gran- ny, for she's yer Mam-my's

Mam-my, Ye can -na shove yer gran-ny aff a bus, Push! Push!

Ye can shove yer ither Granny aff a bus
Ye can shove yer ither Granny aff a bus
Ye can shove yer ither Granny
'Cos she's yer Faither's Mammy
Ye can shove yer ither Granny aff a bus.

Ye can shove yer Uncle Wullie aff a bus
Ye can shove yer Uncle Wullie aff a bus
Uncle Wullie's like yer Faither
A harum-scarum blether
Ye can shove yer Uncle Wullie aff a bus.

Ye can shove yer Auntie Maggie aff a bus
Ye can shove yer Auntie Maggie aff a bus
Auntie Meg's yer Faither's sister
She's naethin' but a twister
Ye can shove yer Auntie Maggie aff a bus

But ye canna shove yer Granny aff a bus
O ye canna shove yer Granny aff a bus
O ye canna shove yer Granny
'Cos she's yer Mammy's Mammy
O ye canna shove yer Granny aff a bus.

46

The Barnyards o' Delgaty

♩ = 104

1. As I cam' in by Tur-ra mar-ket, Tur-ra mar-ket for to fee,

4. I fell in wi' a weal-thy fair-mer, The barn-yards of Del-ga-ty.

Chorus:

6. Lin-ten a-die too-rin a-die, Lin-ten a-die too-rin ee,

8. Lin-ten low-rin, low-rin, low-rin, The barn-yards of Del-ga-ty.

2. He promised me the ae best pair
I ever set my e'en upon;
When I gaed tae the Banyards
There was naething there but skin and bone.

Chorus

3. The auld black horse sat on his rump
The auld white mare lay on her wime;
For a' that I could 'Hup' and crack,
They wouldna rise at yoking time.

Chorus

4. When I gaed to the kirk on Sunday,
Mony's the bonnie lass I see,
Sitting by her faither's side
And winking ower the pews at me.

Chorus

5. I can drink and no' be drunk
And I can fecht and no' be slain
I can lie wi' anither man's lass
And aye be welcome to my ain.

Chorus

6. My cannle noo it is brunt oot
The snotter's fairly on the wane;
Sae fare ye weel, ye Barnyards,
Ye'll never catch me here again.

Chorus

OMB 95

Skye Boat Song

Chorus

Though the waves leap, soft shall ye sleep,
Ocean's a royal bed.
Rocked in the deep Flora will keep
Watch by your weary head.

Chorus

Many's the lad fought on that day
Well the claymore could wield
When the night came silently lay
Dead on Culloden's field.

Chorus

Burned are our homes, exile and death
Scatter the loyal men;
Yet, ere the sword cool in the sheath,
Charlie will come again.

Chorus

The Haughs o' Cromdale

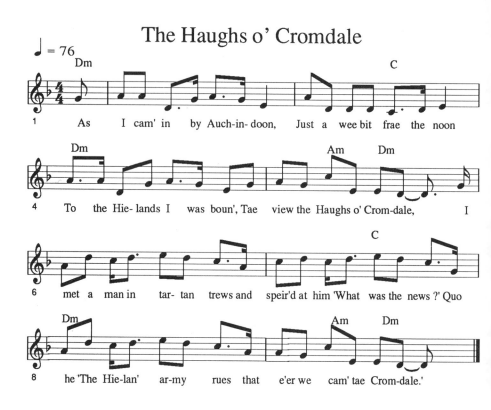

♩ = 76

1 As I cam' in by Auch-in-doon, Just a wee bit frae the noon

4 To the Hie-lands I was boun', Tae view the Haughs o' Crom-dale, I

6 met a man in tar-tan trews and speir'd at him 'What was the news?' Quo

8 he 'The Hie-lan' ar-my rues that e'er we cam' tae Crom-dale.'

'We were in bed, Sir, every man, when the English host upon us cam'
A bloody battle then began, upon the haughs o' Cromdale.
The English horse they were so rude, they bathed their hoofs in Highland blood,
But our brave clans they boldly stood, upon the haughs o' Cromdale.'

'But alas, we could no longer stay, for o'er the hills we came away,
And sore we did lament the day, that e'er we cam' tae Cromdale.'
Thus the great Montrose did say,'Can you direct the nearest way ?
For I will o'er the hills this day, and view the haughs o' Cromdale.'

'Alas, my Lord, you're not so strong, you scarcely have two thousand men,
And there's twenty thousand on the plain, stand rank and file on Cromdale.'
This the great Montrose did say,'John Hielandman, show me the way
For I will o'er the hills this day, and view the haughs o' Cromdale.'

They were at dinner every man, when great Montrose upon them cam'
A second battle then began, upon the haughs o' Cromdale.
The Grant, MacKenzie and Mackay, soon as Montrose they did espy,
Oh, then they fought most valiantly, upon the haughs o' Cromdale.

The MacDonalds they returned again, the Camerons did their standards join,
MacIntosh played a bloody game, upon the haughs o' Cromdale.
The Gordons boldly did advance, the Frasers fought with sword and lance,
The Grahams they made the heads to dance, upon the haughs o' Cromdale.

The loyal Stewarts with Montrose, so boldly set upon their foes,
And brought them down with Hieland blows, upon the haughs ' Cromdale.
Of twenty thousand Cromwell's men, five hundred fled to Aberdeen,
The rest o' them lie on the plain, upon the haughs o' Cromdale.

There was a Wee Cooper

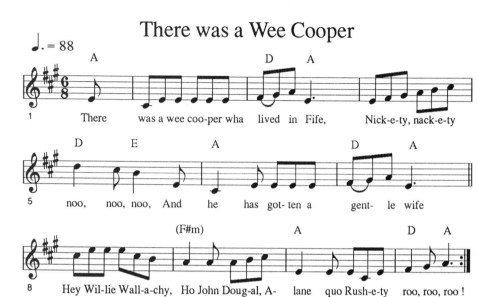

2. She wadna bake and she wadna brew,
   Nickety etc.
   For the spoiling o' her comely hue,
   Hey etc.

3. She wadna card and she wadna spin,
   Nickety etc.
   For the shaming o' her gentle kin,
   Hey etc.

4. The cooper's awa to his woo' pack
   Nickety etc.
   And he's laid a sheepskin on his wife's back
   Hey etc.

5. 'I'll no trash you for your proud kin
   Nickety etc.
   But I will thrash my ain sheepskin.'
   Hey etc.

6. 'O I will bake and I will brew:
   Nickety etc.
   And never think mair o' my comely hue.'
   Hey etc.

7. 'O I will card and I will spin:
   Nickety etc.
   And never think mair o' my gentle kin.'
   Hey etc.

8. A' ye wha hae gotten a gentle wife
   Nickety etc.
   Just send ye for the wee cooper o' Fife.
   Hey etc.

The Trooper and the Maid

♩ = 66

1 A troop-er lad cam' here last nicht, Wi' ri-din' he was wea-ry, A
6 troop-er lad cam' here last nicht, Fan the moon shone bricht an' clear- ly

2 'Bonnie lassie, I'll lie near ye noo,
   Bonnie lassie, I'll lie near ye,
   An' I'll gar a' your ribbons reel
   Or the mornin' ere I leave ye.'

3 She's ta'en his heich horse by the heid,
   An' she's led him to the stable,
   She's gi'en him corn an' hay to ate,
   As muckle as he was able.

4 She's ta'en the trooper by the han',
   An' she's led him to her chamber,
   She's gi'en him breid an' wine to drink,
   An' the wine it was like amber.

5 She's made her bed baith lang an' wide,
   An' she's made it like a lady,
   She's ta'en her wee coatie ower her heid,
   Says: 'Trooper, are ye ready?'

6 He's ta'en aff his big top coat
   Likewise his hat an' feather,
   An' he's ta'en his broadsword frae his side,
   An' noo he's doon aside her.

7 They hadna' ben but an oor in bed
   An oor an' half a quarter,
   Fan the drums cam' beatin' up the toon,
   An' ilka beat was faster.

8 It's 'Up, up, up', an' oor curnel cries,
   It's 'Up, up, up', an' away'
   It's 'Up, up, up', an' oor curnel cries,
   'For the morn's oor battle day.'

9 She's ta'en her wee cloakie ower her heid,
   An' she's followed him doon to Stirlin',
   She's grown sae fu' an' she couldna boo,
   An' they left her in Dunfermline.

10 'Bonnnie lassie, I maun leave ye noo,
   Bonnie lassie, I maun leave ye,
   An' oh, but it does grieve me sair
   That ever I lay sae near ye.'

11 It's 'Fan'll ye come back again,
   My ain dear trooper laddie,
   Fan'll ye come back again
   An' be your bairn's daddy?'

12 'O haud your tongue, my bonnie lass,
   Ne'er let this partin' grieve ye,
   When heather cowes grow ousen bows,
   Bonnie lassie, I'll come an' see ye.

13 Cheese an' breid for carles an' dames,
   Corn an' hay for horses,
   Cups o' tea for auld maids,
   An' bonnie lads for lasses.

OMB 95

He Widna Wint His Gruel

There was a weaver o' the North, and O but he was cruel
O, the very first nicht that he got wed, he sat and grat for gruel
He widna wint his gruel, he widna wint his gruel
O, the very first nicht that he got wed, he sat and he grat for gruel.

'There's nae a pot in a' the hoose, that I can mak' your gruel'
O, the washin' pot it'll dae wi' me, for I maun hae ma gruel
For I maun hae ma gruel, I canna wint ma gruel;
O, the washin' pot it'll dae wi' me, for I maun hae ma gruel.'

There's nae a spoon in a' the hoose, that you can sup your gruel,'
O, the gairden spade it'll dae me, for I maun hae ma gruel.
For I maun hae ma gruel, I canna wint ma gruel
O, the gairden spade it'll dae me, for I maun hae ma gruel.'

She gaed ben the hoose for cakes an' wine, and brocht them on a too'el
O, gy'wa, gy'wa wi' your fal-de-rals, for I maun hae ma gruel
For I maun hae ma gruel, I canna wint ma gruel
O, gy'wa, gy'wa wi' your fal-de-rals, for I maun hae ma gruel

Come all young lassies take my advice and never marry a weaver
The very first nicht we went tae bed, he sat and grat for gruel,
He widna wint his gruel, O, he widna wint his gruel;
O, the very first nicht we went tae bed, he sat and grat for gruel,

OMB 95

The Road to Dundee

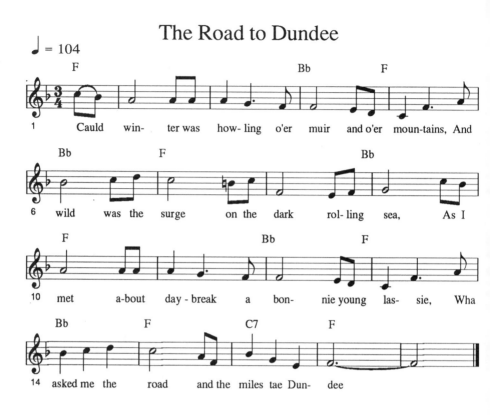

♩ = 104

Cauld win- ter was how- ling o'er muir and o'er moun-tains, And
wild was the surge on the dark rol- ling sea, As I
met a-bout day - break a bon- nie young las- sie, Wha
asked me the road and the miles tae Dun- dee

Says I 'My young lassie, I canna' weel tell ye,
The road and the distance I canna' weel gie,
But if you'll permit me tae gang a wee bittie,
I'll show you the road and the miles to Dundee.'

At once she consented, and gave me her arm,
Ne'er a word I did speir wha the lassie might be;
She appeared like an angel in feature and form,
As she walked by my side on the road to Dundee.

At length wi' the Howe o' Strathmartine behind us,
And the spires o' the toon in full view we could see;
She said, 'Gentle sir, I can never forget ye
For showing me so far on the road to Dundee.'

'This ring and this purse take to prove I am grateful,
And some simple token I trust ye'll gie me,
And in times to come I'll remember the laddie
That showed me the road and the miles to Dundee.'

I took the gowd pin from the scarf on my bosom,
And said, 'Keep ye this in remembrance o' me',
Then bravely I kissed the sweet lips o' the lassie
Ere I parted wi' her on the road to Dundee.

So here's to the lassie—I ne'er can forget her—
And ilka young laddie that's listening tae me;
And never be sweer to convoy a young lassie,
Though it's only to show her the road to Dundee.

OMB 95

My Last Farewell to Stirling

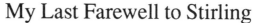

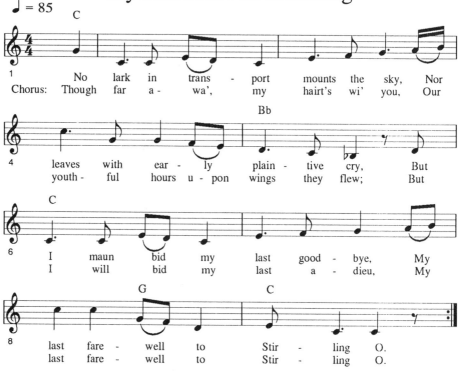

No lark in trans - port mounts the sky, Nor
Chorus: Though far a - wa', my hairt's wi' you, Our

leaves with ear - ly plain - tive cry, But
youth - ful hours u - pon wings they flew; But

I maun bid my last good - bye, My
I will bid my last a - dieu, My

last fare - well to Stir - ling O.
last fare - well to Stir - ling O.

2. Nae mair I'll meet you in the dark,
   Nor gang wi' you to the king's park
   Nor raise the hare oot frae their flap
   When I gang far frae Stirling O.

   Chorus

3. Nae mair I'll wander through the glen
   Nor disturb the roosts o' pheasant hen
   Nor chase the rabbits to their den
   When I gang far frae Stirling O.

   Chorus

4. There's one request before I go
   And that is to my comrades all —
   My dog and gun ye'll keep for me
   When I gang far frae Stirling O.

   Chorus

5. Noo fare ye weel, my Jeannie dear,
   For you I'll shed a bitter tear
   But I hope you'll find some other, dear
   When I am far frae Stirling O.

   Chorus

6. Then fare ye weel, for I am bound
   For twenty years to Van Dieman's Land
   But speak of me and what I've done
   When I gang far frae Stirling O.

Skinny Malinky Lang Legs

♩ = 85

1 Skin-ny ma lin-ky lang legs, um-be-rel-la feet

5 Went tae the pic-tures an' could-nae find a seat. He

9 took the bus hame an' he wid-nae pay his fare. So the

13 rot-ten auld con-duc-tor kicked him doon the stair

OMB 95

Auld Lang Syne

♩ = 85

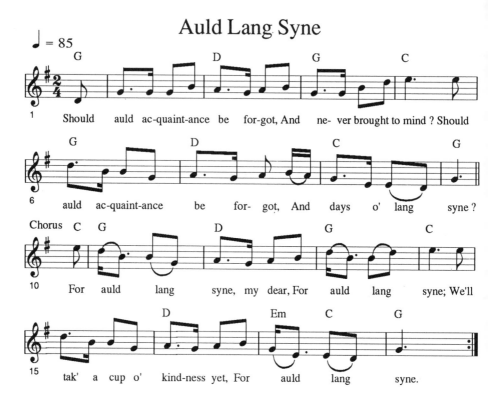

2 And surely ye'll be your pint-stowp !
   And surely I'll be mine !
   And we'll tak' a cup o' kindness yet,
   For auld lang syne.

   Chorus

3 We twa hae run about the braes,
   And pu'd the gowans fine;
   But we've wander'd mony a weary fit
   Sin' auld lang syne.

   Chorus

4 We twa hae paidl'd in the burn,
   Frae morning sun till dine;
   But seas between us braid hae roar'd
   Sin' auld lang syne.

   Chorus

5 And there's a hand, my trusty fere !
   And gie's a hand o' thine !
   And we'll tak' a right gude willie-waught,
   For auld lang syne.

   Chorus

A Brief Guide to the Songs

Although in no way meant to be comprehensive, the following notes will give as far as is relevant and traceable some idea of the background of each song in this volume.

5. THE FOUR MARIES

Mary Stuart apparently had four ladies in waiting: Mary Seaton, Mary Beaton, Mary Fleming and Mary Livingston. This old ballad exists in several formats. Professor Child, the collector, included 28 versions in his collection of 'The English and Scottish Popular Ballads'. Although the tale refers to the subject of infanticide, it appears to have been a very popular moral tale indeed since it was first written in the 18th century. The events surrounding the ballad are rather unclear but are most likely to point to an incident at the Scottish court, where in 1563 a French maid of Mary Queen of Scots was executed. In some versions the king himself is implicated and Mary - moralizingly - explains how she 'hae killed my 'boney wee son . . . . . and well deserved to dee.' The narrative, first-person style of the song is very direct and the tune matches its strength to full effect.

yestreen — last night; the night — tonight; gowd — gold; dule o' — doom/end of

6. DRUMDELGIE

From Ord's 'Bothy Songs and Ballads'. A fine old jaunty Bothy song this, more or less in the form of a farm hands' litany of abuses in his work conditions. The treatment meted out to ordinary farmworkers was harsh and inhuman - in the landlord's eyes these people did not rate much higher than any beast of burden. It took the industrial revolution and the birth of the unions to change all this. Of course now the tide has turned completely and farm labourers cannot be had for love or money in many places.

Wha's kent baith faur an' wide — who's known both far and wide; tae — to; muckle toon — great town; sair — rough/brutal/tough; straik — comb/brush; syne — then; brose — oat or pease-meal mixed with boiling water or milk; gi'en our pints a tie — put our pint vessels away; mull — mill; strait wark — hard/tricky job; sark — shirt; through the fan — whenever we can; neeps — swedes; owsen — oxen; strae raips — straw ropes; queets — ankles; gyaun — going; snaw — snow; ploo — plough; cairting — carting; aft — often; saiddler — whip; weety — damp; maist — most

8. YE BANKS AND BRAES

Written by Robert Burns in 1794 to the tune of 'The Caledonian Hunt's Delight'. The story may reflect the poet's concern regarding Peggy Kennedy,

OMB 95

the young niece of his friend Gavin Hamilton. Burns had stayed with the young girl and he wrote the song 'Young Peggy' for her. Years later on hearing of her predicament brought about by a 'false-hearted lover' he composed this song. This is possibly one of the best known of all Burns' songs.

brae — slope of a hill; aft — often; ilka — every; staw — stole

9. LOCH LOMOND

This song first appears in print in the 1840's. The old tune 'Kind Robin lo'es me' is the air used. The song was originally taken down from 'a poor little boy who was singing on the streets of Edinburgh' in the 1820's by Sir and Lady John Scott. It must have been subsequently 'tidied up' by Lady Scott as in the early printed versions she is credited as the author of the words. The song itself may date back to the 1740's, and refers to the hurried retreat of Prince Charles Edward from the English campaign. It may be that the 'Ye'll take the high road' part of this song has turned into something of a 'musical souvenir of Scotland', but that still cannot take away from the beauty and pathos of this fine song.

braes — river banks; gloamin' — twilight; kens — knows; waeful — sorrow/wailing; greetin' — crying/weeping

10. THE BONNIE HOOSE O' AIRLIE

The air is in Gow's sixth Collection of 1882. The events surrounding this ballad date back to the civil war when the Earl of Airlie (Airly/Airley) fell foul of the covenanters. In 1639, in the Earl's absence, a raid on his house was undertaken by the Earl of Argyle and the mansion was burned to the ground. There appears to have been elements of personal rancour in Argyle's wrath, in any case he certainly did a thorough job: 'he wrought with his own hands, till he did sweate, knocking down the door-posts and headstone of Airley castle'. The lady mentioned was Lady Ogilvy, Airlie's daughter in law, who was asked to look after the place, when according to the song she was sexually harrassed by a 'previously spurned Argyle and forced to show him where the treasures were hidden.'

stane — stone; grat sairly — wept sorely; durst na — did not dare; drury — treasure; plantin' — plantation/estate; mony mae/mony mair— many more

12. O, MY LOVE IS LIKE A RED, RED ROSE

Words by Robert Burns. This is what John Grieg, the editor of 'Scots Minstrelsie' has to say about this well-known song: 'Rough ore, thrown into the melting-pot of Burns's genius, comes out as purest gold.' This song is the result of a lot of improvements and changes, both in the words and the music. The original may have been written by a Lieutenant Hinches. Burns introduced parts of another 'farewell' type song. Although the poem originally was sung to the air 'Major Graham' and later to 'Queen Mary's Lament', it is nowadays married to a modern version of 'Low Down in the Broom'.

13. MINGULAY BOAT SONG
Words by Hugh S. Roberton 1874-1952 (See: 'Lewis Bridal Song' and 'Westering Home') set to a traditional highland air. The author himself supplies 'Lochaber' as a likely origin, but it doesn't really sound like it. My version here differs from Roberton's own arrangement.

14. THE DOWIE DENS O' YARROW
This is one of the grand old ballads from the N.E. of Scotland. Although both words and music may vary in different versions, there is a remarkable consistency in the general theme and the elaborate description of the events. The story told evidently harks back to a period when men's lib had not been heard of yet. The notion of fighting off nine 'gentlemen' to gain the hand of a lady does seem curious today. Not that this makes the song in any way dateable. Some origins have been suggested, but this tale could have taken place anywhere, anytime in the last 400 years or so. Our version here is taken from 'Ord's Bothy Songs and Ballads' (1930). Other versions may be found in the Greig Duncan Folksong Collection (song 215, vol II), and also in 'The English and Scottish Popular Ballads' (song 214) by Francis James Child.

dowie dens — gloomy/(narrow) valleys; marrow — match; ane — one; jimp — bodice

16. HENRY MARTIN
This song really became very popular at the time of the folk-revival of the 1960's, thanks to the singing of Joan Baez, Burl Ives and others. Although the origins of both the words and the tune are vague, some sources point to the true story of Andrew Bardon, a captain of a merchant ship in the 15th century. After his ship was seized by the Portuguese, the Scottish King offered so-called 'letters of reprisal' to Bardon's sons Andrew, Robert and John. In effect this was something of a *carte blanche* to revenge their own losses on the next foreign ship that came along. (These were the good old days, you see!) Bardon, after his first few 'reprisals' developed a taste for this form of legitimate piracy, but eventually incurred Henry VIII's displeasure when he started to attack even English ships as well - while pretending to mistake them for Portuguese merchants.

OMB 95

18. THE DEIL'S AWA' WI' THE EXCISEMAN

Written by Robert Burns. There are two conflicting stories about the origins of this song. In the first and most dramatic, Burns, the exciseman, finds himself awaiting reinforcements from Dumfries before boarding a French brig to impound her cargo. After several hours waiting in the wet salt marshes Burns was getting increasingly impatient and was heard to abuse his colleague Lewars, who had galloped off with the message. One of the waiting men suggested that devil should take Lewars for his pains and that Burns might meanwhile produce a song about the leisurely messenger. Burns allegedly said nothing, but after walking along the shore some time, returned and recited this wonderfully wicked little song. The second and more down to earth version has Burns simply writing the verses for a toast at an excisemen's dinner. It is of course possible that he first wrote it in the marshes and later recited it publicly at the dinner! The tune is 'The Hemp Dresser', first printed in Playford's 'Dancing Master' of 1675.

deil — devil; ilka — every; Auld Mahoun — Old Devil (from Mohammed); mak our malt — make our malt; mony braw — many handsome/many hearty; meikle/muckle/mickle — great/big; ae best dance — best dance ever/still

19. MY DONALD

A fairly recent and permanent contribution to the great folksong cauldron. This song is by Owen F. Hand and simply has the edge on anything else in the way of folkmusic in the sixties. It has all the poignancy and atmosphere only the best of Scottish songs can offer. This moving lament tells of the sorrows of those left ashore while their menfolk were away for considerable periods hunting the sperm whale.

20. A PAIR O' NICKY TAMS

An absolutely daft song with a great lilt to it! Although probably intended to be nothing but a music hall novelty, it has over the years been accepted as part of the treasure chest of Scottish Folksong. This cornkister - or Bothy Ballad - was produced by a G.S. Morris. Nicky tams were leather straps buckled below the knees (a bit like bicycle clips) and were meant as some protection against clouds of dust thrown up during farmwork. The tune is 'Queer folk i' the shaws'.

schweel — school; fee'd me tae the mains etc. — hired me out to the farm(er); pit — put; narrow breeks — tight breeches (pants); tae hap my spinnel trams — to cover my spindly legs; knappin' — shaking (litt. knocking); Baillie loon — servant to the magistrate; gaed on for third — went on for a better position;

breid — bread; eynoo — now; deen — worn; gars — gets/makes; ower fou — too full; fan — when; breist straps — breast straps (from harness); kitchie deem — kitchen maid (dame); clorts a muckle etc. — prepares (litt. scrapes) a big snack for me (of bread or scone); unco — strangely; nane ower lang — none too long; pooch — pouch; muckle gowk — big fool; unco sweer — without feeling like it; lirkit up — rode up/crumpled up

22. LEWIS BRIDAL SONG (*Mairi's Wedding*)
This is a traditional tune taken down by Dr. Peter A. MacLeod (1797-1859) who published four volumes of Scottish songs. This particular song was issued with new words by Hugh S. Roberton (1874-1952), who among other things conducted a very popular choral group of Glasgow singers - the Orpheus Choir. He produced many choral arrangements of Scottish songs. His best known pieces are in his 'Songs of the Isles' published in 1950.

rowan — mountain ash; shielings — huts/cottages - also: summer pastures on the hillsides

23. THE BRAES O' KILLIECRANKIE-O
'The Gaberlunzie Men' from Ayr used to sing a lovely version of this song, which first appeared in Hogg's 'Jacobite Relics of Scotland' (1819-1821). In the year 1689 General Mackay and his army of 4000 Dutch and English troops suffered defeat at the hands of a Highland army led by Claverhouse, the constable of Dundee. More than 2000 of Mackay's men died, while in the other camp the apparently invincible 'Dundee' was shot and killed. It was rumoured that this took a silver bullet to achieve !

whaur — where; bauld — bold; clankie — blow; gled — buzzard (litt. kite); gart — makes; loof — hand; tae shank — to run/leg it; slaes — sloes; deils — devils

24. THE GLENCOE MASSACRE
The massacre of Glencoe, February 13, 1692. It may be argued that this episode in Scottish history would best be forgotten, but perhaps this near-annihilation of a highland clan provides food for thought. Could it not be said that since Glencoe (and certainly before as well), the world has witnessed many similar outrages? Entire villages, town, tribes, sects and countries have been destroyed by robotic military men acting under orders from mentally deficient rulers. ('Befehl ist befehl'- as the Nazis justified their actions). For two weeks captain Robert Campbell and his men stayed with the MacDonalds Clan at Glencoe, were they played cards, drank and generally fraternized with the MacDonalds.

OMB 95

Captain Campbell, himself, through marriage was related to Ian MacDonald, the Clan Chieftain. On Feb. 12, Major Duncanson, Campbell's superior, sent a communication stating that: 'You are hereby ordered to fall upon the McDonalds of Glencoe and put all to the sword under seventy . . . ' The words of this song were printed on broadsheets and in chapbooks, but are probably not older than the 19th century. No great poetic fireworks here - it may have been the effort of a local teacher or literary hack for the benefit of a broadsheet printer.

loured — threatened

26. SCOTS WHA HA'E
Often regarded as the Scottish National Anthem, this song was written by Burns on August 1, 1793. In a letter to his publisher George Thomson he writes: 'There is a tradition which I have met with in many places in Scotland, that it ('Hey Tutti Tatti') was Robert Bruce's march at the battle of Bannockburn.' Burns may have been inspired by his visit to the site of the battle in 1787, when he imagined 'gallant, heroic countrymen coming o'er the hill and down upon the plunderers of their country.'

wha ha'e wi' — who have with; lour — threatening; sae — so

27. THE SCOTTISH EMIGRANT'S FAREWEEL
Words and music are by Alexander Hume (1811-1859), a classically trained musician from Edinburgh. Hume was the author of many Edinburgh-published collections of psalm and hymn books. He later moved to Glasgow where he turned to producing secular songs instead (has Glasgow that effect on composers?), such as his well-known 'Afton Water' and 'My Dear Nell'.

wight — courageous/valiant

28. THE GALLOWA' HILLS
A fine old song resurrected through the medium of that great Scottish singer Jeannie Robertson. The words are by William Nicholson (1783-1849). In 'Nicholson's Poetical Works', it appears as 'The Braes of Galloway,' and is indicated to be sung to the air of 'The White Cockade'. I first heard this song in a pub in Ayr, sung by the Gaberlunzie Men, a popular duo of folksingers, both ex-policemen from Glasgow.

plaidie — shawl; abune — above; anither blaw — another blow; doon fa's a' — litt. 'down comes everything' (when all goes wrong); rock — distaff (with wool or flax attached); reel — spool (for yarn)

30. JOHNNY LAD

A little gem of a 'nursery' song, well-known in Glasgow and other places. This 19th century piece, which includes some interesting Biblical information as well, may have started out as a drinking song.

bawbee — old halfpenny; shoon — shoes; fitba' — football; jyle — jail; focht wi' cuddies' jaws — fought with the jawbone of an ass; louped intae — jumped into; wis oot he wis gey — were out he was very

32. DUNCAN GRAY

Words by Robert Burns. It has been said that the tune of this song was taken down by a musician in Glasgow from the singing of Duncan Gray, a carter. A 'smautty' song of the same name existed long before Burns's time. This is what the poet wrote in a letter to Thomson (1792): 'Duncan Gray is that kind of horse gallop of an air which precludes sentiment. The ludicrous is its ruling feature.' The air may be found in MacGibbon's 'Scots Tunes' (1755). Ailsa Craig is a steep rock in the Firth of Clyde, between Ayrshire and Cantire.

coost — did cast; asklent — aside; unco — very; skeigh — disdainful; gart — made; abeigh — at bay; fleeched — flattered; baith — both; grat — wept; e'en — eyes; blear't an' blin' — bleary and blind; spake o' lowpin o'er a linn — spoke of leaping over a waterfall/torrent; sair — sore; hizzie — young woman; sic — such; na be — not be; crouse — brisk and bold; canty — cheerful

33. THE SUN RISES BRIGHT IN FRANCE

Set to an old Gaelic air, the words are by Allan Cunningham (1784-1842), a much-loved Scottish prose-writer and poet. Cunningham's family moved to Dalswinton on the Nith, just opposite Burns's farm of Ellisland. Although Allan was only twelve years old when Robert Burns died, he was greatly influenced by Burns's personality. Cunningham, although himself a prolific and relatively successful writer remained a humble individual who had a humble and respectful admiration for Scott and the other great names in Scottish literature of the time.

tint the blink — lost the gleam; weets aye my e'e — wets my eye so often; bienly low'd— comfortably flamed; leal — loyal

34. THE FLOWERS OF THE FOREST

Out of the two versions extant, this is the 'modern' and most popular one. Set to

OMB 95

an old harp tune, it first appears in the Skene MS. (c.1630). The new words are fragments of the older song together with parts of 'I've heard them lilting' by Jane Elliot (1727-1805). The song speaks of the battle of Flodden (Sept. 9th, 1513). On that day King James IV, and the cream of Scottish nobility were slain by the troops of Henry VIII. The King, nine earls, fourteen lords, the chiefs of many Highland clans, as well as thousands of nameless rank and file were massacred. The forest alluded to is the district containing the whole of Selkirkshire, parts of Peebleshire, and some of Clydesdale, which at one stage were a favourite hunting resort of the Scottish Kings and nobles. The 'flowers' of the song may refer to the quality of the archers and footsoldiers that came from this forest area.

green loaning — commons; wede — carried off (to their death); buchts — sheepfold; scorning — feigned scolding (teasing); dowie and wae — sorrowful and wretched; nae daffin', nae gabbin' — no fun nor chatting; sabbing — sobbing; ilk ane lifts her leglen and hies her away — each (every) one lifts her milkpail and hurries off; hairst — harvest; bandsters — a party of harvesters; lyart — grizzled/old; runkled — wrinkled; fleeching — cajoling/flattering; swankies — strapping young men; 'bout stacks — around the hay stacks; bogle — hide and seek; dule and wae — alas and woe; aince — once; wan — won

36. THE WINTER IT IS PAST
The air comes from Oswald's 'Caledonian Pocket Companion' (c.1742). Cromek, the editor of many Burns songs found the first eight lines of this song among the manuscripts and accredited Burns with it. It had however been published before in Johnson's 'Museum', where it was mentioned as being of unknown authorship. Interestingly, the bulk of this song is very well known in Ireland, but exists there with an added chorus, providing it with an Irish location: 'And straight I will repair to the Curragh of Kildare, for it's there I'll find tidings of my dear'.

37. OH CHARLIE, O CHARLIE
From Ord's 'Bothy Songs and Ballads' of 1930. A song of farm life and work, where the farmer himself is taking a holiday and instructs his foreman on how to run the place in his absence.

loosin' — unloading; colin' — making haycocks; dee't — does it; aneath — underneath/below; a-hyowin — a-hoeing; keepit — kept

38. FAREWELL TO FIUNARY
The words of this song were written by the Rev. Norman MacLeod, of

Glasgow, who was known as 'Caraid nan Gaidheal' or the Highlander's Friend. The air precedes the words and was taken from the Gaelic song 'Irinn drinn u horó', composed by Allan McDougal, better known as 'Ailean dall,' or Blind Allan.

Eirich agus tiugann O — Gaelic for: Arise and let us go

40. LEEZIE LINDSAY
The tune is an old Highland melody. The first four lines were contributed by Burns for the compilation of Johnson's 'Museum'. Further verses of it were printed in Jamieson's 'Popular Songs and Ballads' of 1806. The song also appears in the Kinloch MSS, where it is called 'Donald of the Isles'.

dinna ken — don't know; maun — must; sae — (here) if;

41. COULTER'S CANDY
Robert Coultart, a travelling confectioner active around the turn of the century, hawked his sweets around the country fairs and markets in the Borders. Like all hawkers, the man's sales pitch included a snatch of a song, which in his case was the first verse of this ditty.

greetin' — crying; bawbee — a bob/sixpence; puir — poor; affa' — awfully; rickle o' banes— pile/heap of bones; sooking — sucking; roon' — round; croon — crown; rin doon — run down/away

42. BONNIE STRATHYRE
Kenneth McKellar may not have been a folk singer but I make no apologies for having cherished the scratchy old record on which he sings it. It's a grand old-fashioned song that should not be sung too fast.

lang simmer — long summer; gane doun — gone down; mony — many; wad — would; rowans — fruit of the mountain ash; e'en — eyes; gang sodgerin' — go soldiering; aye — always; bigg — build; scen — scent; sodger — soldier

44. TURN YE TO ME
This air is an old Highland melody. The words are by John Wilson (1800-1849) who published a collection of 'Songs of Scotland' (London 1842). Wilson's book sold well, especially because he always sang his songs at lecture-recitals, which he gave up and down the country. To great acclaim, he also toured around with 'Scottish Entertainments' such as 'Jacobite Songs', 'A night wi' Burns', and 'Mary Queen of Scots.'

OMB 95

Mhairi dhu — Gaelic for dark (haired) Mary

46. YE CANNA SHOVE YER GRANNY AFF A BUS
Just a sweet (more like acid!) old Glasgow nursery rhyme, set to the strains of 'She'll be comin' round the mountain'.

47. THE BARNYARDS O' DELGATY
From Ord's 'Bothy Songs and Ballads'. Like 'A Pair o' Nicky Tams' and 'Drumdelgie' these are old bothy ballads or 'cornkisters' dating back to the 19th century. These songs and ballads were wholly occupied with the trials and tribulations of farmworkers. Many of the songs found their way into the vaudeville stage around the turn of the century. Versions of this particular song abound - some of them running into as many as 16 verses. The condensed (and more singable) version printed here is taken from the singing of Ewan MacColl.

fee — hire oneself out to a farmer; ae best pair — very best team (of ploughing horses); wime — belly; fecht — fight; cannle — candle; brunt oot — burnt out; snotter — wick

48. SKYE BOAT SONG
The version given here is Harold Boulton's set of words, which have superseded the original lyrics written in 1893 by Miss Margaret Bean of Piperton Mains, near Brechin. The tune is an old Hebridean rowing-song. The song relates the famous escape of Prince Charlie in the winter of 1745-6, when with his Flora Macdonald and a few devoted Highland boatmen he managed to cross a stormy and raging sea between South Uist and Skye.

claymore — broad sword

50. THE HAUGHS O' CROMDALE
The historical facts of this song have to be taken with a sizeable grain of salt. But why spoil a good yarn with a bit of truth ? First printed in Hoggs Jacobite Relics. The Greig-Duncan collections reveal no less than five versions, two of them from taken down from singers, the first being a Mrs Gillespie and the second source was a blind Aberdeen street singer in 1909. Cromdale is near the town of Grantown-on-Spey.

haughs — level ground/river-meadow land; trews — trousers; speired/spiered — enquired/asked

52. THERE WAS A WEE COOPER

(Child 277) 'The Wife wrapped in Wether's skin' is another version of this song which ultimately may have sprung from a folk tale - 'The wife wrapped in Morrell's Skin.' In the story and all the songs, the theme is that of a husband dealing with his slothful wife. In all versions the woman receives a *hiding* (so that's where the expression comes from!) and re-emerges perfectly reformed. The Wee Cooper o' Fife is probably a 19th century music hall adaptation.

woo' pack — herd of sheep; I'll no — I won't

53. THE TROOPER AND THE MAID

From Prof. Child's collection (nr. 299). According to him there are several other ballads of a trooper and maid, and many appear related. Some of the verses may be found back in songs like 'The Bonnie Lass of Fyvie', 'Pretty Peggy' and others.

reel — whirl; heich — tall; oor — hour; curnel — colonel; boo — bow/stoop; haud — hold; heather cowes — twigs of heather; ousen bows — cattle yokes; carles — men/fellows

54. HE WIDNA WINT HIS GRUEL

A song well-enough known in Aberdeenshire, but I failed to locate it in print in any of the major collections. It bears the stamp of vaudeville all over it. perhaps one of Harry Lauder's forebears came up with this one.

gruel — porridge; dae — do; maun — must; canna wint ma — can't go without my; grat — wept; ben — into; gy'wa — go away

56. THE ROAD TO DUNDEE

One of my personal favourites, this is perhaps one of the most artless and plain songs in the Scottish repertoire. Seldom were lyrics and tune so well matched. In these days when most people are unused to take in a longish ballad like this one, it always manages to compel one's attention. There is an Irish counterpart - at least of the sentiments of this song: - 'Sweet Carnlough Bay' which is set to a different tune. Our Scottish song appears in many formats and set to different tunes. Other versions, close to the one given here may be found in Ord's 'Bothy Songs and Ballads,' Gavin Greig's Collection, and 'Songs and Ballads of Dundee' by Nigel Gatherer.

muir — moor; canna' weel gie — cannot (well) tell you; wee bittie — small bit; speir wha — inquired who; toon — town; gowd — gold; ilka — every;

OMB 95

sweer/sweir — reluctant/unwilling; convoy — accompany

58. MY LAST FAREWELL TO STIRLING
From the singing of Ewan MacColl and others. MacColl got his versions from
Willie Mathieson of Castleton, near Banff and Jamie Taylor of Fyvie. This is
one of many transportation songs. These songs are highly illustrative of the
instant and merciless 'justice' of the past (perhaps not just the past!). The theft
of a cabbage or poaching some fish would have been quite sufficient to ensure
a one-way ticket to Australia or Van Dieman's Land (Tasmania).

oot frae their flap — out from their lair

59. SKINNY MALINKY LANGLEGS
A great old favourite skipping rhyme with more than a touch of sardonic big-
town humour in it. Alighting from Scottish buses seems a hazardous
occupation — see: 'Ye Canna Shove your Granny Aff a Bus'.

60. AULD LANG SYNE
Although Burns is generally credited with this song, he only added the third
and fourth verses to an already existing song of the same name. Burns wrote:
'The air is but mediocre; but the following song, the old song of the olden times
and which has never been in print, nor even in manuscripts, until I took it down
from an old man's singing, is enough to recommend any air.'
Thomson, Burns' publisher, set the words to another better-fitting air: 'I fee'd a
lad at Michaelmas', also known as 'The Miller's Wedding', 'The Miller's
Daughter', and 'Sir Alexander Don's Strathspey'. Although 'Lang Syne' owes
much to the literary and musical intercessions of Burns and Thomson, it
continues to shine and charm us with its timeless simplicity. Some songs
always engender this warm feeling of being there because we needed them. If
Silent Night produces that same feeling at Christmas time, 'Lang Syne' will do
this on New Year's Eve all around the world and more particularly at Scottish
gatherings.

auld lang syne — of long ago/lit. 'old long since'; pint-stoup — pint-size
tankard; brae — the side of a hill; pu'd — pulled; gowans — daisies; mony —
many; paid'led — paddled; dine — dinner-time; braid — broad; hae — have;
fiere — friend/companion; gie's — give us; gude — good; willie-waught —
draught (of drink)